FARM ANIMALS

CHICKENS

Written by
Eliza Nodes

Genius Kid

sales@northstareditions.com | 888-417-0195

Library of Congress Control Number:
The Library of Congress Control Number is available on the Library of Congress website.

ISBN
979-8-89471-055-6 (library bound)
979-8-89471-075-4 (paperback)
979-8-89471-113-3 (epub)
979-8-89471-095-2 (hosted ebook)

Printed in the United States of America
Mankato, MN
012026

Written by:
Eliza Nodes

Edited by:
Sadie Hallworth

Designed by:
Ker Ker Lee

All facts, statistics, web addresses, and URLs in this book were verified as valid and accurate at time of writing. No responsibility for any changes to external websites or references can be accepted by either the author or publisher.

Photo Credits – Images courtesy of Shutterstock.com, unless otherwise stated.

Cover – Nynke van Holten, cynoclub, Eric Isselee, oksana2010, cynoclub, New Africa, cameilia, Dora Zett, Ton Ponchai, Galyna Syngaievska. 2–3 – khathar ranglak, Majna. 4–5 – Aksenova Natalya, Tsekhmister. 6–7 – pets in frames, Aksenova Natalya, natthawut ngoensanthia. 8–9 – Sonsedska Yuliia, Eric Isselee. 10–11 – Ton Ponchai, GPPets, Eric Isselee, cynoclub. 12–13 – INTREEGUE Photography, Galdric PS, Nick Beer, Ton Ponchai. 14–15 – New Africa, Nattika, FabrikaSimf, NinaM, DenisMArt, BearFotos. 16–17 – Suranto W, malshkoff, KOOKLE, Oleksandr Lytvynenko, Nick Beer. 18–19 – LightField Studios, Pordee_Aomboon, Julia Zavalishina. 20–21 – Oleksandr Lytvynenko, Noiel, 1EYEman, snezhana k, Galdric PS, Erwin Bosman. 22–23 – Sriya Pixels, Sonsedska Yuliia, Nynke van Holten, ADOKAVAK, Manbetta, Litvalifa.

CONTENTS

Page 4	Chickens
Page 6	Body of a Chicken
Page 8	Face of a Chicken
Page 10	Breeds of Chickens
Page 12	Life on the Farm
Page 14	How People Use Chickens
Page 16	From Chick to Chicken
Page 18	Looking After Chickens
Page 20	Believe It or Not!
Page 22	Are You a Genius Kid?
Page 24	Glossary and Index

Words that look like <u>this</u> can be found in the glossary on page 24.

CHICKENS

When you picture a chicken, what do you see?

What color are the chicken's feathers? Is the chicken sitting on eggs?

Chickens are birds. They are warm-blooded. They also have a backbone, wings, and feathers.

DID YOU KNOW?

Male chickens are called roosters. Female chickens are called hens.

Chickens are omnivores. Omnivores are animals that eat plants and meat.

Most chickens are domesticated. They are kept by humans. Most chickens live on farms, but some people keep them as pets.

BODY OF A CHICKEN

Chickens have wings. However, they can't fly very well or for very long.

Hen

The feathers on a chicken's neck are called hackles. Chickens raise their hackles when they are uncomfortable.

Roosters have long, curved tail feathers. Hens do not.

Chickens don't have feathers on their legs. They have four toes. Three toes point forward and one toe points backward. They use their claws to scratch and dig in the ground.

FACE OF A CHICKEN

Chickens' eyes are on the sides of their heads. They have excellent eyesight, which helps them spot small insects to eat.

Chickens' beaks are made of keratin. This is the same thing human fingernails are made of. Chickens use their beaks for grooming and eating.

Chickens have ears on the sides of their heads. The ears are protected by feathers.

The red parts on a chicken's face are called combs and wattles. These parts help chickens keep cool.

BREEDS OF CHICKENS

There are many different chicken breeds. Breeds are created and controlled by humans to have certain characteristics.

Rhode Island Reds are one of the most popular types of chicken. They have red-brown feathers and bright red combs.

Sussex chickens come in eight colors, including brown, white, and speckled.

Barnevelder chickens come in many colors. The most common have black and golden feathers.

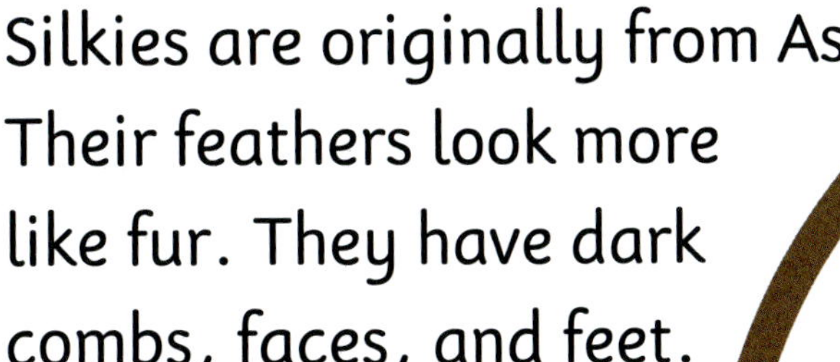

Silkies are originally from Asia. Their feathers look more like fur. They have dark combs, faces, and feet.

Japanese Bantams are small with short legs and low wings that often touch the ground.

LIFE ON THE FARM

Chickens need warm, dry places to live. Farm chickens usually live in barns.

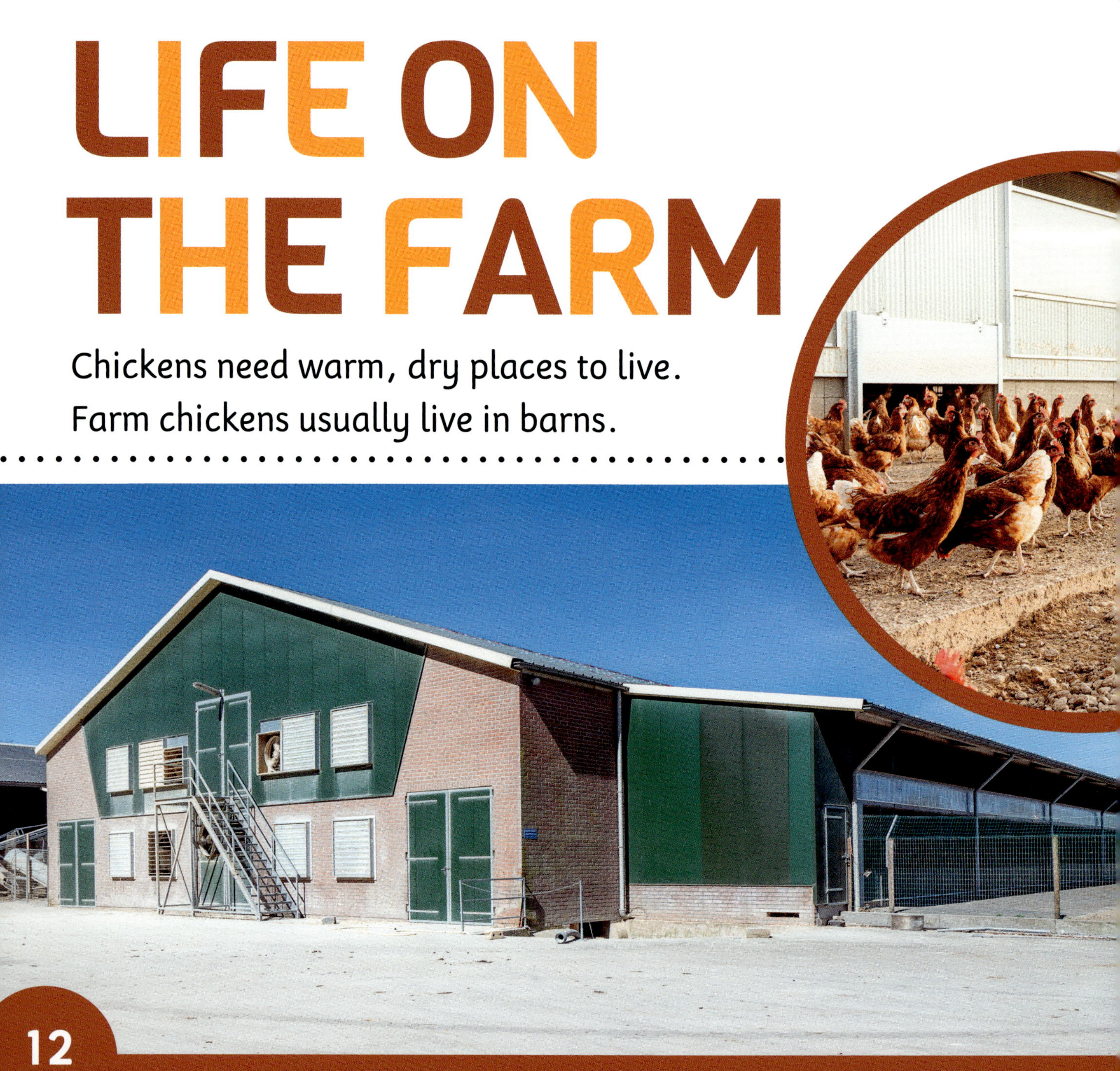

Some barns have small doors called pop holes. Chickens can go outside through these doors.

Pet chickens or small flocks sometimes live in small houses called coops.

Chickens eat specially-made chicken food or pellets. This food is mostly made of grain, corn, or soybeans. It has vitamins to keep chickens healthy.

DID YOU KNOW?
A group of chickens is called a flock.

HOW PEOPLE USE CHICKENS

Most chickens and chicken eggs are made into food.

Chicken meat can be eaten in many ways, such as chicken nuggets. Chicken eggs can be eaten once cooked. Raw eggs are also used to make foods such as mayonnaise or cakes.

Some people keep small flocks of chickens in their backyard so they can use their eggs.

Some people keep chickens as pets. Pet chickens need a safe outdoor space to play in. They also need a coop or shelter to sleep and rest in.

FROM CHICK TO CHICKEN

Baby chickens are called chicks. Mothers lay eggs and sit on them to keep them warm. On farms, eggs are often placed inside an incubator to keep them warm.

Chicks hatch from their eggs by making small holes in the eggshell with their beaks.

Hens start laying eggs at around 18 weeks old. Most farms keep egg-laying hens until they are two or three years old. Backyard chickens may keep laying for five to ten years.

Chickens raised for meat usually live for around five to eight weeks.

LOOKING AFTER CHICKENS

If a hen isn't healthy, she won't lay many eggs. Any chicken that is ill can't be used for food.

Farmers and owners need to have their chickens checked by a vet if they have any health problems.

DID YOU KNOW?
A vet is a doctor for animals.

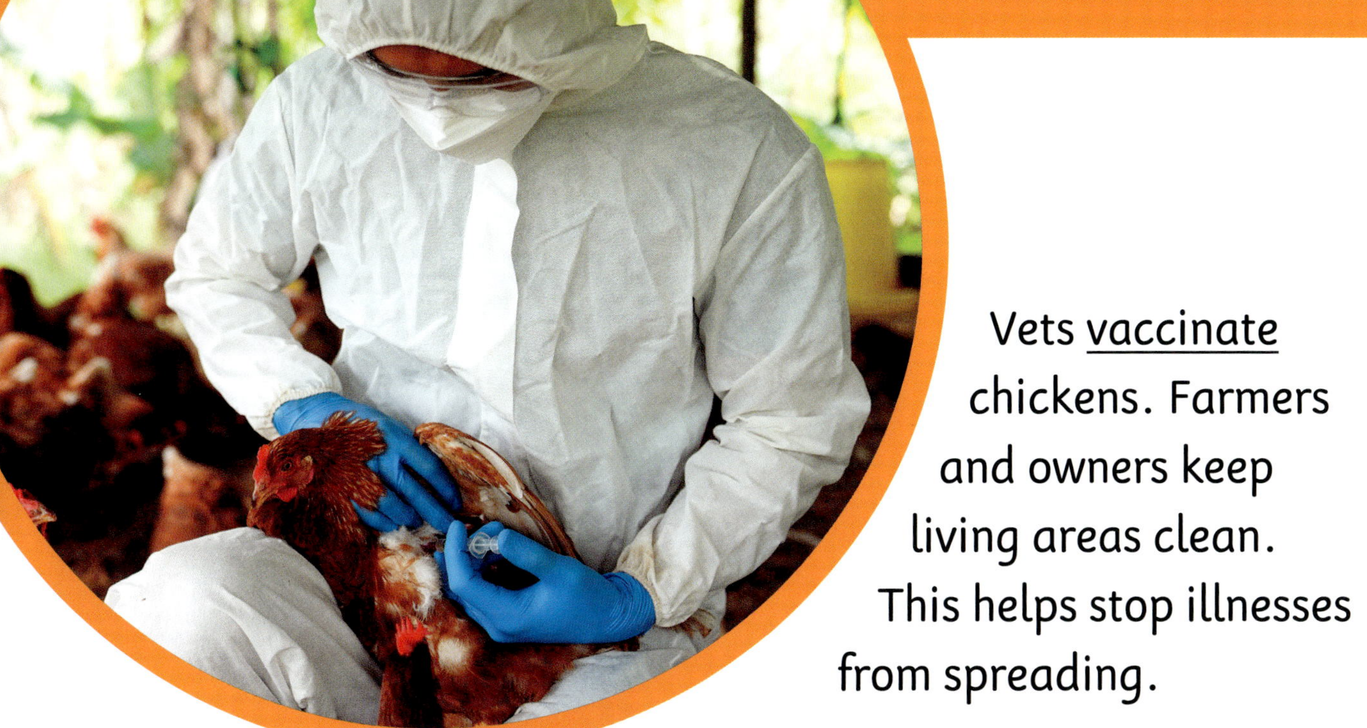

Vets vaccinate chickens. Farmers and owners keep living areas clean. This helps stop illnesses from spreading.

Vets help farmers make sure the flocks get everything they need.

BELIEVE IT OR NOT!

Chickens are one of the closest living family members to dinosaurs. All birds, including chickens, have ancestors that include the Tyrannosaurus rex.

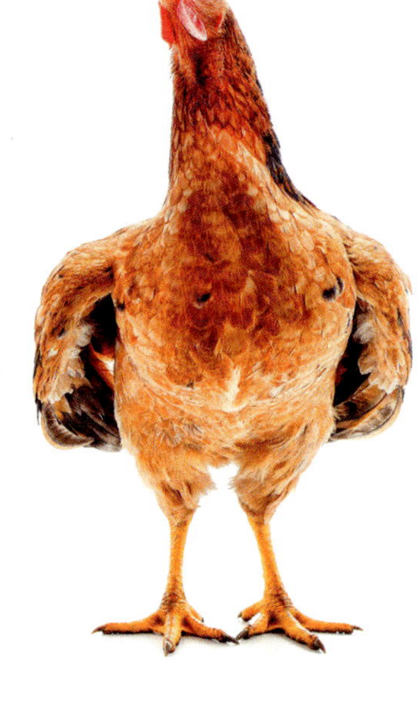

Chickens are very smart. They can learn from one another. They can also solve puzzles such as picking up a cup with food hiding underneath.

Chickens have good memories. They can recognize chicken and human faces, even when they haven't seen them for a long time.

Chickens can dream! Scientists know this because of the ways chickens' eyes move while they sleep.

ARE YOU A GENIUS KID?

Now you know many things about chickens, so you can amaze your friends and family! But how much of it can you remember? Let's find out what you have learned.

Check back through the book if you are not sure.

1. What is the word for an animal that eats plants and meat?
2. How do chickens show they are uncomfortable?
3. Chickens are one of the closest living family members to ______?

Answers:
1. omnivore
2. by raising their hackle feathers
3. dinosaurs

GLOSSARY

ancestors people or animals in a family who lived long before the current family members

breeds groups of animals that are bred to have similar characteristics

characteristics features of a living thing that help to identify it

grooming when an animal brushes and cleans its coat, fur, or feathers

hatch to come out of an egg

incubator a warm box designed to support the growth and development of a young animal

vaccinate to inject medicine into a person or animal to protect against a disease

vitamins substances needed for normal and healthy growth

INDEX

chicks 16
combs 9–11
coops 13, 15
eggs 4, 14–18
farms 5, 12, 16–17
feathers 4, 6–7, 9–11
hens 4, 6–7, 17–18
pets 5, 13, 15
roosters 4, 7
wings 4, 6, 11